SOUND Artistry
INTERMEDIATE METHOD
for BASSOON

PETER BOONSHAFT & CHRIS BERNOTAS

in collaboration with

JOSHUA ELMORE

Thank you for making *Sound Artistry Intermediate Method for Bassoon* a part of your continued development as a musician. This book will help you progress toward becoming a more able and independent musician, focusing on both your technical and musical abilities. It offers material ranging from intermediate to advanced, making it valuable for musicians at various experience levels.

The many instrument-specific exercises in this book will help to support your personal improvement of techniques on your instrument, focusing on skills that may not always be addressed in an ensemble or in other repertoire. You will notice there are many performance and technique suggestions throughout the book. This wonderful advice has been provided by our renowned collaborative partners, as well as the many specialist teachers we worked with to create this book.

Sound Artistry Intermediate Method for Bassoon is organized into lessons that can be followed sequentially. As you progress through each lesson, it is a good idea to go back to previous lessons to reinforce concepts and skills, or just to enjoy performing the music. Exercises include Long Tones, Flexibility, Major and Minor Scales (all forms), Scale Studies, Arpeggio Studies, Chromatic Studies, Etudes, and Duets, as well as exercises that are focused on skills that are particular to your instrument. You will notice that many studies are clearly marked with dynamics, articulations, style, and tempo for you to practice those aspects of performance. Other studies are intentionally left for you to determine those aspects of your musical interpretation and performance. This book progresses through various meters and every key. Once a key has been introduced, previous keys are interspersed throughout for reinforcement and variety. In the back of this book you will also find expanded-range scale pages and a detailed fingering chart.

We wish you all the best as you continue to develop your musicianship, technique, and artistry!

~ Peter Boonshaft and Chris Bernotas

Joshua Elmore is the principal bassoonist of the Fort Worth Symphony Orchestra. He has performed with orchestras around the world, including The Chineke! Orchestra, New York Philharmonic, Saint Paul Chamber Orchestra, Dallas Symphony, Oregon Symphony, Charleston Symphony, and Baltimore Symphony.

Before joining the Fort Worth Symphony Orchestra, Joshua completed his Professional Studies Certificate at the Colburn School in Los Angeles under the tutelage of Richard Beene. He is a Kovner Fellow graduate of The Juilliard School, where he studied under Judith LeClair.

alfred.com

ISBN-10: 1-4706-6652-9
ISBN-13: 978-1-4706-6652-1

Instrument photos provided courtesy of Jupiter Band Instruments/KHS America

Lesson 1

1   **LONG TONES**—*The top-left pinky key used when playing a low E♭ is also known as the resonance key. This key is added with certain notes to improve the resonance and sound. The resonance key should be used on top-space G in the bass clef and on some notes in the tenor/higher register. In the fingering chart at the back of the book, you will find the notes that require the use of the resonance key.*

2   **LONG TONES: CHROMATIC**—*In this exercise, utilize the pinky F♯. That is the fingering for the F♯ in this register.*

3   **FLEXIBILITY**

4   **C MAJOR SCALE AND ARPEGGIO**—*For all scale exercises that are written in octaves, practice each octave separately and then as a two-octave scale and arpeggio.*

5   **C MAJOR SCALE STUDY**

6   **ARPEGGIO STUDY**

7 ETUDE—*Play all etudes slowly with a steady tempo and good tone quality before speeding up. Always keep a good tone in mind and perform with musicality.*

8 ETUDE

9 ETUDE—*Practice this etude with two-bar phrases and then four-bar phrases.*

10 DUET

Lesson 2

FLICKING, or VENTING, is a technique used on the bassoon to avoid cracking on notes in the tenor register. This involves the momentary pressing (or "flicking") of one of the two or three (depending on your instrument) upper thumb keys for the tenor A (top line of the bass clef) B♭, B, and C. Flicking will be indicated with a circle (○) and should be used at the start of the note, then released while the note is held. Stepwise slurs to those notes may not require flicking. Flicking for tenor D should be used only when approached from a slur. Tenor C♯ does not require flicking. For rapidly repeated flicked notes, you may try holding the flick key down. Flicking ensures that the sound is consistent throughout all registers.

continued on
next page

16 CHROMATIC SCALE

17 CHROMATIC SCALE ETUDE

18 ETUDE

19 ETUDE—*When playing in the low register, keep a relaxed, dropped jaw while making an "oh" shaped oral cavity. After playing this etude as written, create or improvise a new ending for the last two measures.*

All notes that require flicking have been marked with a ○ in this lesson. Apply this technique as needed for all exercises throughout the book.

6

Lesson 3

20 **LONG TONES**—*Remember to always have proper posture, embouchure, and hand position to promote performing with a beautiful tone.*

21 **FLEXIBILITY**

22 **F MAJOR SCALE AND ARPEGGIO**—*Sing or hum these notes before playing them. Internalizing the pitch will help develop your aural skills.*

23 **F MAJOR SCALE STUDY**—*Be sure to play this slowly at first, to ensure technical facility.*

24 **ETUDE**

25 **ARPEGGIO STUDY**

26 **ETUDE**—*Ensure that the articulation in the lower register of the instrument is crisp and clear. Play this etude at a slower tempo, if needed.*

27 **DUET**

Lesson 4

28 **D MINOR SCALE**

29 **D MINOR SCALE STUDY**

30 **ETUDE**

31 **ETUDE**—*Work toward clean slurs and clarity with flicked notes. Leave the whisper key early to ensure that the flick key is depressed.*

32 **DUET**—*Work toward matching each of the musical elements in this duet for a unified performance.*

33 **ETUDE**—*Play this etude with an eighth-note pulse until the rhythm is accurate. Then, transition to the dotted-quarter-note pulse. Aim for a round and full legato sound. Experiment using a Da syllable for this articulation.*

Lesson 5

34   **ETUDE**—*Keep the articulation light and bouncy. Don't let the accents change the intonation.*

35   **ETUDE**

36   **ETUDE**—*Practice this etude at a slower tempo to help you keep an even rhythm and clear articulatons. Once you are comfortable, increase the tempo. Don't forget to flick where needed.*

37 ETUDE

38 DUET

39 ETUDE—*Perform this etude with a beautiful, singing style. Work on a consistent airflow through the slurs.*

12

Lesson 6

40 **FLEXIBILITY**—*Ensure all slurs are clean between the registers.*

41 **G MAJOR SCALE AND ARPEGGIO**—*Gs in the middle register should include the E♭ key or resonance key for sound and stability.*

42 **G MAJOR SCALE STUDY**—*Using manuscript paper or notation software, compose a new scale study that you think is even more challenging.*

> When playing in the higher register, sometimes the bassoon part may be written with a **TENOR CLEF**, which is one of the C Clefs. It is good practice to become familiar with notes in this clef. Middle C is notated on the fourth line up from the bottom.

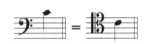

43 **RANGE EXTENSION**—*Make sure you don't play flat on notes in the tenor register, as this is a common issue on bassoon.*

44 **RANGE EXTENSION**

45 INTERVAL STUDY

46 ETUDE

47 ETUDE—*Practice this etude with two-bar phrases and then four-bar phrases.*

48 ETUDE—*Emphasize the difference between the notes that have staccato and accent markings.*

Lesson 7

49 FLEXIBILITY

50 E MINOR SCALE

Natural   Harmonic

Melodic   Arpeggio

51 E MINOR SCALE STUDY

52 ETUDE

Majestically ♩ = 88

53 ETUDE—*Ensure air is moving through changes in register to help with smooth, legato articulations.*

Adagio ♩ = 66

54 **ETUDE**—*Make sure there is a clear difference in style between the sections marked "lightly" and "legato." Practice making the character of the music different and obvious.*

55 **ETUDE**—*After successfully playing this etude, seek guidance from a teacher for ways you can refine your performance.*

56 **ETUDE**—*Make sure you use good air support throughout this etude.*

Lesson 8

57 **FLEXIBILITY**

58 **B♭ MAJOR SCALE AND ARPEGGIO**

59 **B♭ MAJOR SCALE STUDY**

60 **ETUDE**—*If this exercise is not rhythmically even at the dotted-quarter-note pulse, try setting your metronome to the eighth-note pulse of ♪ = 180.*

61 **ETUDE**—*Be creative with the musicality of this etude by altering and adding your own dynamic markings.*

62 DUET

63 G MINOR SCALE

64 G MINOR SCALE STUDY—*For a clear, articulate sound, use more air and move your tongue as little as possible. Less is more.*

65 ETUDE—*Remember, using more air and less tongue movement will help with the clarity of the sound.*

Lesson 9

GRACE NOTES are ornaments that are performed before the beat or on the beat, depending on the musical time period, style, context, and notation. The last example below shows how unslashed grace notes would be performed in the Classical period. Listen to music from various historical periods and notice the different approaches to the performance of grace notes.

Most often performed before the beat

Classical period, no slash. On the beat (in time).

66 **GRACE NOTES**—*Play these grace notes just before the main note.*

Precisely ♩ = 120

67 **ETUDE**

Moderato ♩ = 80

68 **ETUDE**—*An appoggiatura is a grace note without a slash that is played on the beat. In this exercise, measures 1 and 5, as well as measures 3 and 7, would be played the same.*

Cantabile ♩ = 72

69 **ETUDE**

Lightly ♩ = 96

70 **ETUDE**

Andante ♪ = 96

71 ETUDE—*Remember to use flicking for a clean and crisp sound.*

72 ETUDE—*Record your performance of this etude. Recognize the personal musical growth you have made from when you sight-read the piece. Think about the technical and musical ways your performance has improved. Do you hear a difference?*

73 ETUDE—*Practice this etude slowly to focus on technique and fingerings. Once you are comfortable, increase the speed.*

Lesson 10

74 **LONG TONES**—*Make sure the pitch remains stable throughout changes in dynamics.*

75 **FLEXIBILITY**

76 **ETUDE**

77 **ETUDE**

21

78 CHROMATIC SCALE

mp cresc.   *f* decresc.   *mp*

79 CHROMATIC RANGE

mp cresc.   *f* decresc.

mp cresc.   *mf*

* Use the low E♭/resonance key for these notes.

80 MAJOR SCALE RANGE

mp ——— *f* decresc.   *p* ——— *mf*

81 DUET

Andante ♩ = 108

mf

mf

Lesson 11

82 **FLEXIBILITY**

83 **D MAJOR SCALE AND ARPEGGIO**—*Practice this slowly, at first, to ensure an even sound across the entire instrument.*

84 **D MAJOR SCALE STUDY**

85 **ETUDE**

86 **ETUDE**—*Even though this etude is marked "sempre staccato," make sure you have a rounded staccato articulation.*

continued on next page

87 **ETUDE**—*When playing* ♪♪, *make sure you keep a sixteenth-note subdivision in mind. They should not have the feel of triplets.*

88 **ETUDE**—*After performing this etude, discuss the various elements of the musical work with a peer or teacher.*

89 **ETUDE**—*Make sure the second note of a slurred group is not clipped.*

Lesson 12

90 **FLEXIBILITY**—*Practice at a slow tempo to ensure good intonation and technical facility.*

91 **B MINOR SCALE**

92 **B MINOR SCALE STUDY**

93 **B MINOR SCALE STUDY**

94 **DUET**

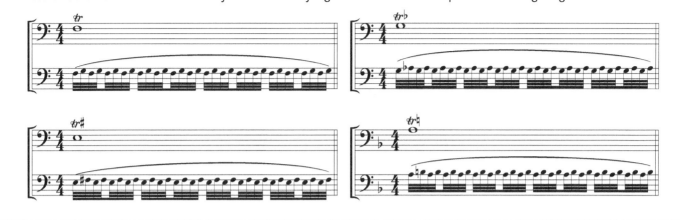

95 TRILLS—*Use your metronome to ensure an even and consistent rhythm.*

96 TRILLS—*Practice this exercise to ensure your trills are played evenly. Once you are comfortable with this exercise as written, try playing it in cut time (♩=160).*

97 TRILLS—*Practice measures 1–5 at a slow tempo to reinforce muscle memory, gradually increasing the tempo. This exercise will help ensure that your trills are played evenly. Keep your fingers close to the bassoon. The less movement you have, the better, especially as notes get faster.*

98 ETUDE—*Depending on the style or historical context, a trill may start with an upper neighbor as shown here. Practice these trills with and without the upper neighbor. Also, grace notes are often used at the end of a trill. This ornament is also known as a nachschläge.*

Lesson 13

99 FLEXIBILITY

100 Eb MAJOR SCALE AND ARPEGGIO

101 Eb MAJOR SCALE STUDY

Andante ♩ = 88

102 ETUDE

Andantino ♩ = 90

103 ETUDE—*Try various articulation patterns for the first four measures of this etude.*

Allegretto ♩. = 80

104 **DUET**

Lesson 14

105 LONG TONES

Slowly ♩ = 60

106 FLEXIBILITY

107 C MINOR SCALE

Natural · Harmonic

Melodic · Arpeggio

108 C MINOR SCALE STUDY

Moderately ♩ = 100

109 ETUDE—*Pay close attention to the notes in the lower register, as they tend to be sharp. Keep an open throat and think of the syllable "oh" when playing.*

Larghetto ♩ = 60

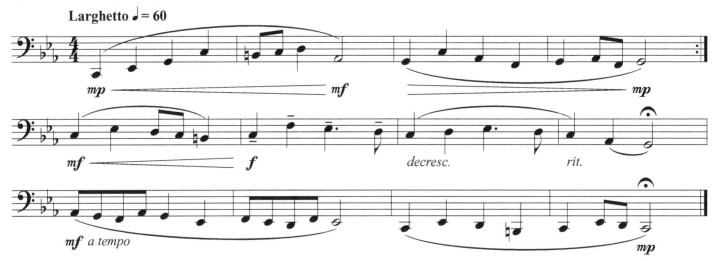

110 **DUET**

111 **ETUDE**—*Try to exaggerate the dynamics in this etude. They help the phrases move forward.*

112 **DUET**—*While playing duets, both performers must listen critically to evaluate and adjust intonation.*

Lesson 15

113 **FLEXIBILITY**

114 **A MAJOR SCALE AND ARPEGGIO**

115 **A MAJOR SCALE STUDY**

Moderately ♩ = 80

116 **ETUDE**

Moderately ♩ = 80

117 **ETUDE**—*Pay special attention to the measures that do not contain slurs. Keep the notes smooth and connected.*

Cantabile ♩. = 60

118 LONG TONES—*These notes tend to be very sharp. Practicing with a tuner will help with your intonation.*

* Include the low C♯ key when playing E in this register. It provides stability to the pitch.

119 F♯ MINOR SCALE

120 F♯ MINOR SCALE STUDY

121 ETUDE

Lesson 16

122 **DUET**—*Remember to flick, where appropriate. Also, when playing* ♫, *remember to think of a sixteenth-note subdivision.*

124 **DUET**—*What musical elements in this duet make it engaging? How does the form contribute to the musical work?*

125 **ETUDE**

Lesson 17

126 FLEXIBILITY

127 Ab MAJOR SCALE AND ARPEGGIO

A **TURN** or **GRUPPETTO** is an ornament that involves playing the written note, followed by the note above it, returning to the original note, then playing the note below it, and finally ending on the original note.

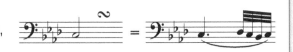

128 Ab MAJOR SCALE STUDY

Adagio ♩= 72

129 Ab MAJOR SCALE STUDY

Moderato ♩= 112

130 ETUDE

Andante ♩= 80

continued on next page

131 F MINOR SCALE

132 F MINOR SCALE STUDY

133 ETUDE—*Exaggerate the dynamics in this etude. Make sure you do not change pitch when the volume increases or decreases.*

Lesson 18

134 LONG TONES

Slowly ♩ = 60

135 FLEXIBILITY

136 E MAJOR SCALE AND ARPEGGIO

137 E MAJOR SCALE STUDY

Moderately ♩ = 100

138 ETUDE

Andante ♩ = 108

139 ETUDE—*Make sure you play three even notes with each beat grouping. Do not shorten the third note.*

Adagio ♩. = 60

140 C♯ MINOR SCALES

141 C♯ MINOR SCALE STUDY

142 ETUDE

143 DUET

38

Lesson 19

144 FLEXIBILITY

145 ETUDE

146 ETUDE

147 ETUDE

148 **DUET**

Presto ♪ = 176

149 **ETUDE**

Moderato ♩ = 112

150 **DUET**—*Use critical listening to improve the performance of all musical elements in this duet.*

Adagio ♩ = 66

40

Lesson 20

151 **ETUDE**—*Work toward a musical performance. Keep the slurred groups very smooth.*

152 **DUET**

153 **ETUDE**

42

157 **ETUDE**

158 **ETUDE**—*Make sure you recognize the difference between sixteenth notes and sixteenth-note triplets.*

159 **DUET**

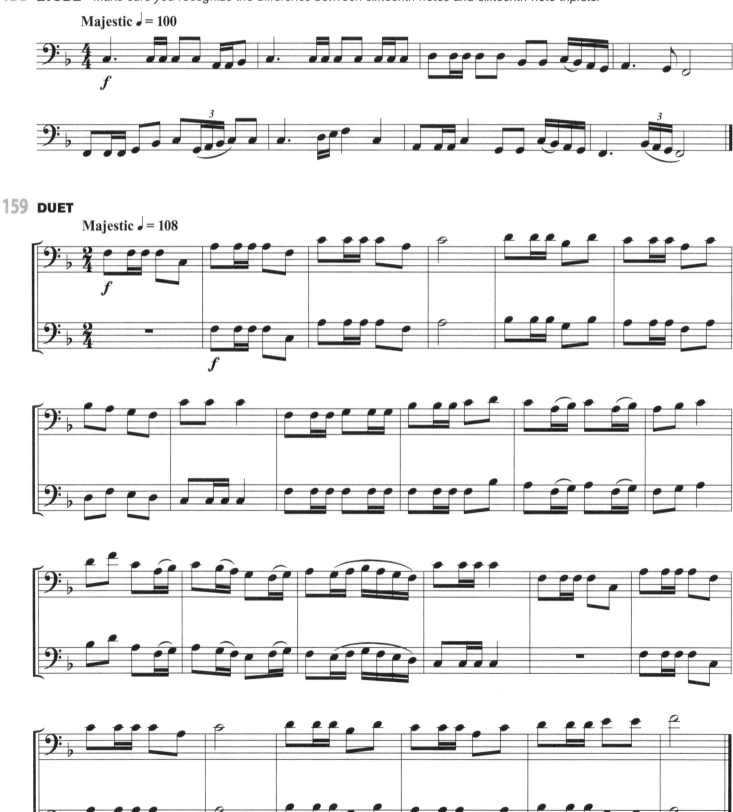

Lesson 21

160 FLEXIBILITY

161 Db MAJOR SCALE AND ARPEGGIO

162 ETUDE

Adagio ♩ = 66

163 ETUDE

Andante ♩ = 100

164 Bb MINOR SCALES

165 ETUDE

Adagio ♩ = 66

44

Lesson 22

166 LONG TONES

167 B MAJOR SCALE AND ARPEGGIO

168 ETUDE

169 ETUDE

170 A♭ MINOR SCALE (*enharmonic spelling of G♯ minor*)

171 ETUDE

Major Scales

C MAJOR

F MAJOR

B♭ MAJOR

E♭ MAJOR

A♭ MAJOR

D♭ MAJOR

G♭ MAJOR

C♭ MAJOR

G MAJOR

D MAJOR

A MAJOR

E MAJOR

B MAJOR

F# MAJOR

C# MAJOR

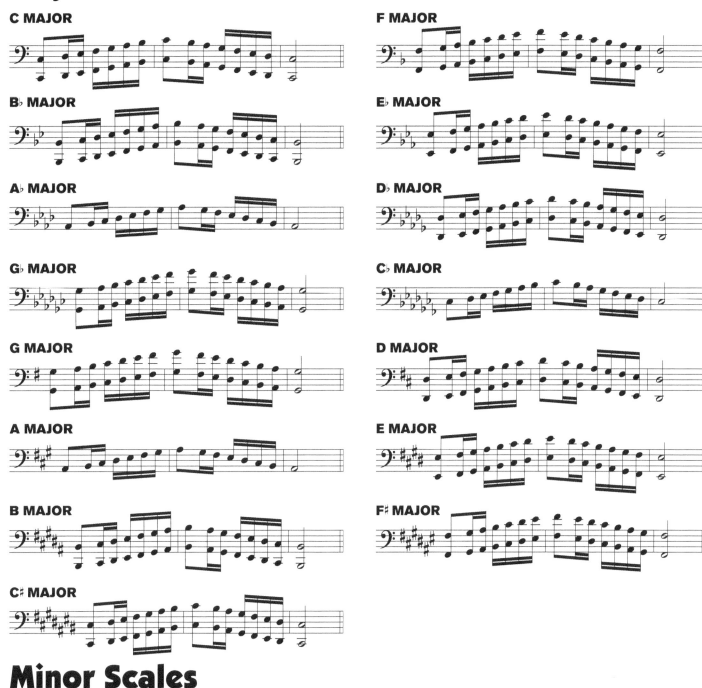

Minor Scales

A MINOR
Natural   Harmonic   Melodic

D MINOR
Natural   Harmonic   Melodic

G MINOR
Natural   Harmonic   Melodic

C MINOR
Natural   Harmonic   Melodic

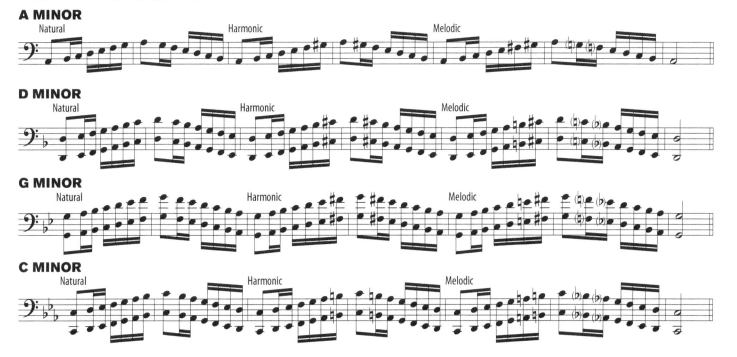

Bassoon Fingering Chart

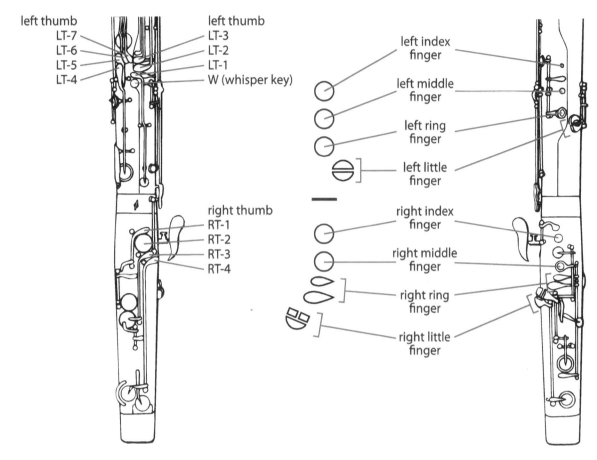

left thumb
LT-7
LT-6
LT-5
LT-4

left thumb
LT-3
LT-2
LT-1
W (whisper key)

right thumb
RT-1
RT-2
RT-3
RT-4

left index finger
left middle finger
left ring finger
left little finger

right index finger
right middle finger
right ring finger
right little finger

○ = open
● = pressed down
◒ = half hole covered
LT = left thumb
RT = right thumb

Flicking, or venting, is a technique used on the bassoon to avoid cracking on notes in the tenor register. This involves the momentary pressing (or "flicking") of one of the two or three (depending on your instrument) upper thumb keys for the tenor A (top line of the bass clef) B♭, B, and C. Flicking will be indicated with a circle (○) and should be used at the start of the note, then released while the note is held. Stepwise slurs to those notes may not require flicking. Flicking for tenor D should be used only when approached from a slur. Tenor C♯ does not require flicking. For rapidly repeated flicked notes, you may try holding the flick key down. Flicking ensures that the sound is consistent throughout all registers.

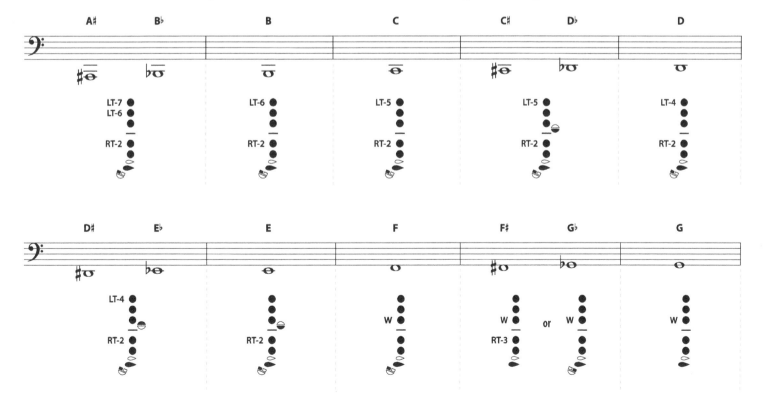

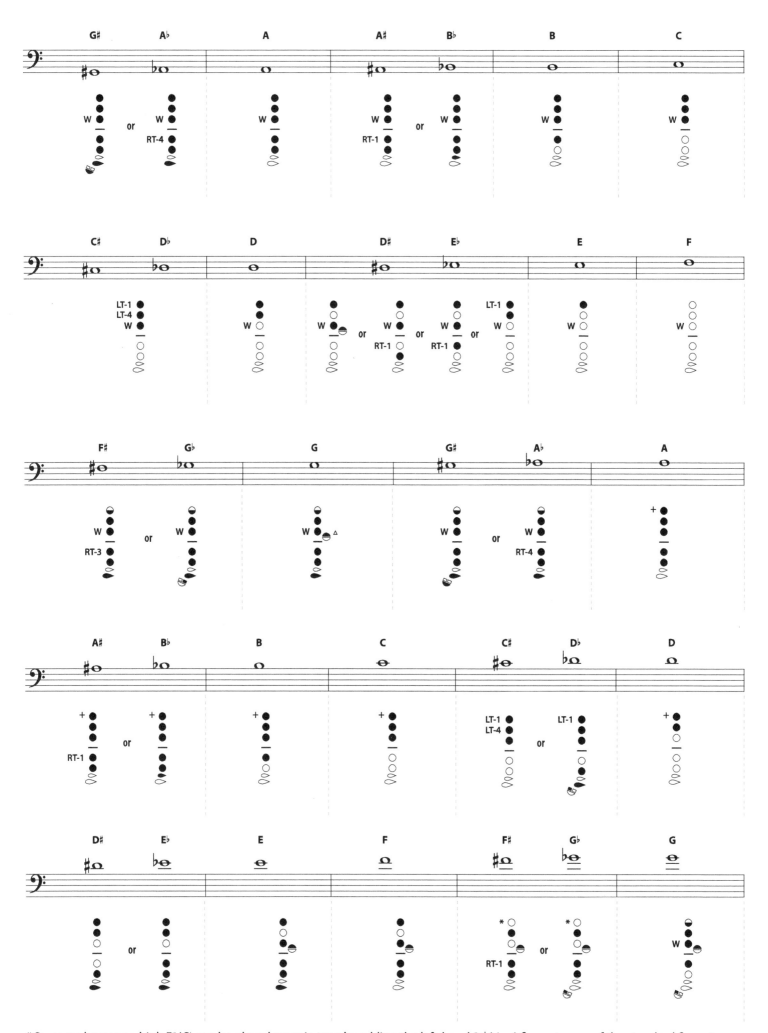

*On some bassoons, high F#/G♭ can be played more in tune by adding the left-hand 3rd (ring) finger to one of the standard fingerings.
+The stability of this note can be improved by touching or "flicking" LT-2 or LT-3 at the beginning of the note.
△Either left pinky can be used depending upon the intonation of the instrument.